Middle Class American Proverb

MIDDLE CLASS AMERICAN
-PROVERB-

JOHN DAVIS JR.

Negative Capability
PRESS
MOBILE, ALABAMA

ISBN 978-0-942544-12-1
Library of Congress Control Number: 2014949383

Negative Capability Press
62 Ridgelawn Drive East
Mobile, Alabama 36608
(251) 591-2922

www.negativecapabilitypress.org
facebook.com/negativecapabilitypress

TABLE OF CONTENTS

THE LAND

THE ANCESTORS

THE SON

The Lovers

The Heirs

The Elder

ACKNOWLEDGEMENTS

THE LAND

The Meaning of Wauchula

"Buzzards' Roost," the old-timers muttered,
recalling the sun-trodden cowhands before them:
Hearty Hardee County folk who knew
too well those pasture scavengers'
oily black feathers, scale-crusted skulls –
turkey vultures awaited free carcasses
from dead-limbed, dirty-mossed vantage points.

"Ibises' Flight," the scoutmaster explained,
pointing to a Seminole dictionary:
Rhythmic shushes of white tapered wings unified
in the Audubon beauty of postcard Florida –
slender-sleek, sickle-beaked graceful birds
crossing, caressing an orange-dusk horizon.

In the end, it became what we made it:
A brittle death-and-desertion existence,
or accumulated desires flying onward –
the nightmarish scrape of cold beaks on bones,
or the light, smooth sound of our dreams' ascent.

Broken History

Our farmhouse's thick crystal doorknobs
captured the light of a sepia age handled
by forefathers' soil-worked palms,
mothers' pricked fingertips.

A tentative turner, uncertain of things
fine and fragile, in childhood I tested
each slow and spectral rotation, rounding
hallway sunlight in antique hours' glass.

The day I broke one off, I cried
as color and sparkle trickled
out, leaving a hard and lifeless chunk
reflecting my hand, magnifying my crime.

No tape, no glue would ever bring it back:
A relic relegated to the dark
drawer of a mahogany box:
our tabled sewing machine.

Old Florida Upstairs

Life in a lowdown flat land means
          there's nowhere to go but up.

Our attics store the rising heat
          and just-in-case leftovers:

Hurricane season's window boards,
          former follies and fascinations –

avarice's aftermath among
          rat poisons and pointed rafters.

Now and then, a sin-curious child
          will trespass, take a wrong step, crash

through the drop-ceiling panels, hang
          on to hot and splintery cross beams

while beneath, guilty legs and feet flail
          into calm, conditioned air of futility

pouring from pure white vents connected
          to silver, filth-laden passageways –

ductwork overhead whispering nothings'
          assurances: Everything is fine, fine, fine…

Hanging Sheets at her Late Parents' Place

She likes their smell, she says:
king-sized unfitted linens dried
in farm fashion – clothesline, sun.
At her childhood home where no one lives,
she still takes in the everyday mail, dusts
the crystal, checks the ice bin.
Half an hour northwest, her grown-up house
clicks and hums its modern sounds –
static in her southeastern absence.
Light wind ripples her bone-colored bedclothes,
waving them like farewell handkerchiefs
or white flags of final surrender.

The Left Farm

There's a lot he misses these days:
That view from the barntop
as color warms into the crops,
the hanging diesel smoke cranked
from an elderly red tractor,
a low, humming groan at the pump
where the well sends strong-smelling
sulfur water through irrigation
lines, down rows of emerald,
and past a lone, age-painted
farmhouse: sitting, waiting
for his return, his touch
inherited and learned from proud
generations of ancestors.
His blood and hands and head
ache for the land, the tasks before:
before this time and state,
before the man who toils
without tilling for a living.
There's a lot he misses these days.

Winter Homestead Chores

Our orange grove sand is more like ash
this season in your absence.
It swallows my footsteps, giving up
clouds of charcoal grey with each
heavy-treading impact burying
my shiny, city-slick boots in memories
of extractions, plantings, countless harvests.

I check the crops' water pump, flush the main line
as you would have done to clear buildup,
and find it an awkward, forced gesture,
waste its only real accomplishment.
Looking back, my singularly paired tracks
seem detached, darkened circles; foreign pits
in this barren, fertile land awaiting new years.

Everglades Requiem

Everything's opposite
of how it should be here:
Dark egrets trace a bright swamp
full of alien Asian once-
pet pythons – captives released
by well-meaning misunderstanding.

Sawgrass teeth spaces grow wider,
trying to sustain their smile while crooked
snakes infest each gap, growing fatter
off native species, ill-equipped victims
of wide jaws and expandable bellies
they pass through, large lumps consumed
by the unexpected unfamiliar.

Skinned knees of Bald Cypress protrude
their injuries above water-level,
exposing the hurts we all feel –
scraped, scratched, shat-upon spires –
reminders of a swallowed ecology,
a time before airboats and outsiders.

Hometown Ekphrasis

Aerial photo in commission chambers, circa 1981

Yesterday's Kodachrome:
glass and steel life
in bodies, the giving
city spreads, uncurls
its fingers. Industrial
isthmuses offer a hand
among the local lakes.

Some days, it welcomes:
its digits gesture
outward, summon
those beyond, "Come here;
you've got to see this."

Others, it punishes:
never fistlocked in anger,
but broad and swift, it
delivers consequence, over-
turns the water tables.

Always, it rescues:
pulling upward
from doubtful whitecaps
around fishing boats,
it lifts the masses
who, in return,
place beams, drive nails.

End Weekend

Our lake is silver
on the cusp of evening
as it is waiting

for sunset, nightfall,
a thousand blind mosquitoes
making black blacker.

Here we are, a lone
boat trolling toward our dock
where God's finger trails

and our wake both stop.
The surface cools to midnight
blue – that good-bye hue

preceding the stars
that navigate our earthbound
vessels to Monday.

THE ANCESTORS

Handcestry

My hands are older today than I remember.
Overnight, they've seasoned into my grandfather's:
one rigid blue vein ridging each index finger
like long-repaired irrigation lines running
our grove rows in black-kneed toolbox summer.

Cut, splice, clip, patch, plug, cap – he taught it all
using that pointer I've inherited, the same one
that gestured during after-work naps. Jobs done,
directions kept flowing – "That's it. Right there."
Age-mottled, earth-brown digits twitched instruction.

Those lines remain – pulsing, delivering
life even after the pump has quieted,
its cycles complete. The soil is filled and grateful.

Why I Won't Fish on Sunday

Commandment Number Four
from Granddad: Remember
Big Roberta Mae Fletcher
and her tall orange Nehi.

She'd skipped service that day
and gone down to the bank
of Peace River, cold drink
relaxing beside her.

As she sullied her hook
with a solemn cricket,
a fat yellowjacket
lit on her bottle's mouth.

Casting her quiet bait,
she went for refreshment
and caught hell instead:
fiery stings in her throat.

They found her swollen shut
on Monday – no prayer,
no hope for revival,
save one black bass struggling

at the end of her line,
detached, released to live.

The Short End

Not quite right: that green garden hose
his hardened hands carefully coiled
into place, there by the barn
when workdays ran out of steam.

Slicker models rolled downtown
in hardware stores boasted
brass fittings on both ends.

Not his: Joined solely at spigot,
and like an adopted stray cat,
had its far end chopped off—

giving the poor thing just length
to water a back flowerbed
or show all the kids how
a real farmer takes a drink.

As older grandchildren, they'd learn:
There was only so much
a single-jointed hose could do,
yet on his land, his time,
it did so irreplaceably.

Evening Watering

My summer bedtime meant flowerbed time
for my grandfather. I could hear him
just outside my window: a clearing
of his throat, then that faucet squeaking
forth a rush of soon-to-be bucket water

poured in measured streams around our begonias.
Old-fashioned, deliberate method: nature
meeting nurture in cautious doses.
His creaking metal pail tilted incremental loads –
soft dark splashes onto near-night earth.

The calm and conservation of evening
watering gave him gentle purpose:
An intentional inefficiency, this
giving of living liquid supply
until the galvanized steel rang dry.

Rebuilding Project

Once a great quail hunter, the old man now
with splotching eyes and cinching hands tears down
his former bird-dog pens to clear space
for the pine wood and plastic greenhouse:
a home for his late wife's tropical orchids.

Yesteryear's common canines get replaced
by the warm damp air of rarest flora.
Quiet new growth supplants past death-fetchers
as the whisper of overhead irrigation reigns
over the snaps and snarls of a younger time.

Water and food dishes become clay pots
and stillness rules where excited motion
once dominated – all teeth and tails.
Xylem and phloem instead transport noiseless
life to and from hushed and splendid blooms.

Closing the door of his new creation,
shutting off water and memory, he
pads his path back to the cob-webbed
living room where no conversation remains –
one last obedient animal commanded: Stay.

Mule Pie

A stubborn-sweet southern woman known
for cobblers, casseroles, and covered dishes
made by traditional hand: my grandmother.

Her soft, bleached flour-white palms, when rolled, turned
toughened, tanned horsehide brown, hardened slow
by heat from lifetime love-labors of hearth

like "mule pie:" long strips of leftover crust,
crisped and sugared, given to favorite
grandsons who persisted, endured as she had

the cold of those moments before reward
made better through warmth and expectation:
baked time-lines sprinkled with simple cinnamon.

Incomplete Farm Chore #5

Wound through chicken wire's hexagonal holes,
the field-mouse-fattened rat snake trapped itself.
Three days it had rigored between the posts,
and today Grandma said, "Go cut it a-loose."

She handed me a throw-away butcher knife,
almost forgotten in the drawer's back shadows.
"And watch the smell," she added, nothing more.

Its eyeballs distended from six-sided sockets
followed my blade without moving or blinking
away the drinking horseflies, the chewing black ants.

Curved out from the fence, its scale-spreading belly
stuck hard among twisted wire, no longer hungry.
It crept up on me: that mangled death-odor
uncoiled after my first meat-spilling strike.

Leaving it hanging, I tossed the knife,
wiped my eyes, approached the porch, assured
myself: Crows will finish the job tomorrow.

His Legacy

Your struggling farmer-artist father
copied Rockwells from Saturday
Evening Posts, Rembrandts borrowed
from gilt-spined Britannicas.

Bright Americana and Blue Boys,
his chugging tractor heart pulsed color
through machinery-dinged fingers; rugged
strokes, master shadows for your mother.

Today in your remote woodshop, you paint
miniature houses cut and pasted
in familiar, unspoken desire:
mountain cabins, grand plantations

seen someplace other than here, where
imitation's inspiration remains.

Laundry Grading

My English-teacher father loved ironing.
Morning ritual: shirt inspection, assessment
made with a head shake and frown before
laying out the Oxford cloth like some horribly wrong
test essay ready for a starch-and-steam sentence,
punishment for grievously flaw-laden garments
in serious need of proofing and editing.
Hot flat black triangle: corrector of errors,
severer and swifter than any red felt-tip pen.

In minutes he'd be creased, seamed, and pressed into perfect
MLA format – pants panels punctuated by pleats
and half-inch, college-ruled margins outlining
his arms in starkest, sharpest, cleanest blank space
created with heat and deliberate precision.
His pendulum necktie marked seconds passing
over a gleaming brass belt buckle,
seemingly saying with each silk swish,
"Time's up. Pencils down. Pass your work to the front."

Father-Son Hunting

What the mind fathoms become its phantoms
in the grey ambivalence of morning –
riddles in the pre-dawn fog, conundrums
of weather, nature conveys a warning:

A cock crows somewhere beyond the treeline.

Between you and me, there is less distance.
Our deer stands are barely a mile apart
along the same reddish creek. Difference
is harder to see in November dark.

An autumn-yellow sun begins to rise.

In your nearby green pastures, this year's sheep
remain unslaughtered, fatted and waiting
for a pair of gunshots to break their sleep,
signaling Harvest initiating.

Morning preyers: two hawks circle above.

Horseshoes

All the luck had run out of that sad arc –
a tacked antique above the barn's back door.
Not a U lifting praising prongs heavenward,
but a frown downturned and painted to hide
rust from an age of long-deceased mares,
corrosion of fortitude and fortune.

In the pre-passing months, Bob threw heavy
horseshoes with older men at the downtown pits.
Hurling curved metal with long farm-boy arms,
he remembered Iowa – its scythes and cycles:
a cool dark barn floor awaiting new crops,
and the corn rows' beckoning green whisper.

Black Rock Hike

For Jerry

Off the trail, we reached that drop-off –
a fifteen-foot wooded ledge shortcut
down toward camp. You'd made it,
looking back up with an old-shouldered shrug:

I can't catch you this time, son.

Nothing from my one decade of life – not
diving boards, barn roofs, or haylofts
with your upstretched arms below them –
had prepared me for this moment of self:

You're too big. You'll just have to jump.

Abandoning ten years' trust-teaching
to favor faith in my own young frame,
I launched an awkward, jarring slalom,
a downward pitch and scrape, grabbing for trees.

Your breath-held silence was amplified by wind.

Knee-deep leaf colors cushioned my descent –
a perilous, proving-ground plunge into nature
apart from man, toward new manhood
found in a north Georgia wilderness Fall.

Souvenir

My great-grandfather Ab, a whip-maker for Florida Crackers,
would have laughed at that cheap Cherokee toy – braided fake
cowhide, the craft store kind, tipped with sueded paper.

He could have shown me the whistle and break of air
over scrub cattle's unfatted haunches. Like leather
men of his generation, he knew business's whir and pop.

Before wars, prickly pear and palmetto prairie spread
snake nests over backcountry trails, sidewinding
toward market in a dust-streeted, matchstick wood town.

It is 1988, a century too late for his lessons.
I would rather be Indiana Jones with my campground friend Jack.
In a day, the toy will be garbage – wound around Carolina pine,

yanked from its balsa handle, it adds a sad tail to woods
once owned by displaced natives, lost and rugged forefathers.

THE SON

The Words I Hate and Why

*"A poet is, before anything else, a person who is
passionately in love with language."*
–W. H. Auden

Summer
The airport is bustling
with wall-to-wall people
and he is there again.

Bubblegum
He blows it full of hot,
sticky, empty man air
and it pops, expelling

Lies
"Maybe next time," he says.
"One day you'll understand.
Here, have some gum; it's good."

Mustache
Little pink bits are caught
up in its black forest –
webs, all tangled and torn.

Terminal
"London, Tokyo, Prague…"
Atlanta, I finish.
Another foreign land.

Departure
My sister is taken
by him. Her blue eyes wane
farther, smaller, swallowed.

Medicated Youth

Regular, but not normal:
Morning and night Phenobarbital
doses supplied by Pete's Pharmacy, kept
in a half-hexagonal amber bottle, black-capped,
imprisoning thicker maroon-tinted liquid.

"Time for Mr. Pheeny," my mother would chime,
as if personification would cure
the ugliness of it all. Then came
her incantation, chanted over loaded
stainless steel care-carried ounces:

"One spoony-spoony,
Two spoony-spoonies,
Three spoony-spoonies…"

Saccharine, smile-spoken words like that sweet air
sound before a hammer blow to a nail head.
My gullet burned bitter as rivulets
of the unkind fluid coursed downward, inward,
ensuring no seizure would pay us an unfriendly visit.

Everyday episodes of epileptic
childhood measured in milliliters
of neurological Castor Oil –
An AM/PM ritual reminder
that stuck in our family's throat.

The Tongue is a Flame

...no man can control.
-- James 3:6, 8(a)

Because it got in the way,
the tongue was always the worst part.

I'd gnaw it bloody raw, swollen
during those night seizures.

Tooth-sized, spit-filled wounds
made village idiot speech:

Guttural utterance thick
with liquid breath and rattle.

Cured by time and ice,
my punctured, heart-rigid muscle,

bit and rudder healed could tell
again its clear and eloquent curses.

Asperger's Syndrome: Day Fifteen

Some days, the thoughts are too much.

My mind is a Mason jar full of marbles:
all beautiful, prismatic, unique, but excessive.
When shaken, it clacks harmonious dissonance:
five hundred perfect spheres all shrieking
to be freed from their transparent trappings,
sent rolling onto the blank page of earth.

This one I shall release for you today, observer:
a deep crimson cat's-eye with a fine streak of white
meant to be studied, admired, held up to the light
and marveled at before its return, sealed tight
in its fragile, crystalline container.

Hold me, love me, cherish me while you can
it cries, knowing its own unfortunate fate:
one day too soon, we'll lose every one of them
underneath the creaking antique armchair,

and no one will bother to look there, in the dark.

North Room Bedtime

Pulling up covers without good-nights, my brother and I
stayed alert for figures in the dark ceiling panels:
block soldiers made of six squares – head, shoulder-arms, waist,
leg stubs, split. They never went anywhere; stuck, reliable
in those high white-gone-black places every night.

We stared them down closer to us, keeping our gazes
so long there the room shook around those chosen
panels and frames – tremors of sight and shadow.
Strained and sorrowless tears forced our eyes to sleep.

Lacklight made us wonder: what shape men would we be?
Who would look for us when the current was off?
Would they embrace assuring geometry – forms
fixed, unshifting – or something three dimensional?

Afternoon Ingredients

Wasps' Nest:

> Tucked under bright green banana tree leaves,
> overhanging the neighbors' chain-link corner
> fence, it formed danger-temptation we sought.
> As penned-in city boys full of longing
> for somethings exotic, tropical, wild,
> and acceptably deadly, it promised an end
> to our desperate bedroom boredom and grey,
> plain-faced lives on the block between
> north-running railroads and a southbound river.

Baseball Bats:

> We planned to piñata that swarm of red-
> striped threats with fiery Louisville Sluggers,
> then run faster than hell away, away
> from the angry crazed buzzing onslaught
> of stinging nature-bullets, back to the known,
> mundane safety provided by parents'
> simple, sad, suburban single-stories
> that never knew adventure madness
> or the proud pink war-welts of daring.

36

Fraterville Central

Being your handlebar passenger demanded
white-knuckle balance and helmetless faith
that you would never steer me wrong.

Bigger, you always saw ahead of me,
avoided cracks and jolts in your paper-boy route
you knew would hurtle me haywire.

Not built for two, our bike betrayed us once:
Your foot slipped off the pedal, we fell
lopsided and laughing in the Laytons' lawn.
We spit-shook and swore our secrecies.

Visiting your facility most Thursdays,
they buzz me in from the outside light.
Wrist-thick metal bars divide our conversation.
I bring you the news: Family, Home, Promises.

Where Our Tunnels Went

We liked to glamorize
those two metal culverts
supporting the road into town
as "tunnels" replete with treasure:
buried pirates' gold and reptiles.

We ventured into those holes
closest home almost daily,
swapping off routes and dirt
like so many battered favorite
toys used and loved by us both.

Returning from a day's plunder,
we had to compare to brag—
bottle caps to squirrel skulls,
pebbles to marbles,
buccaneer booty for certain.

One day, we just reached the end:
we found the city waiting
with vehicles, jobs, and girlfriends
sucking us out of separate,
mutual adventures.

Yet I never drive over those
bridged road sections without
wondering: what boys could be
swapping tales underneath
while my car passes above.

Merry Summer

Stomachache medicine's intense pink:
that ice cream truck on our side of town
had been rescued from the junkyard. Salvation
on summer days: snow cones and drumsticks.

None of us understood, though, why it played
Christmas carols – dinged speaker's warped slow
sound waves: Jingle Bells, Silver Bells, Let It Snow,
yuletide leftovers crackling through July.

Damp dollars and sweaty quarters in hand
for Astro-pops, push-pops, anything cold;
our tiny voices chorused a too-high window,
pleaded with our summertime Santa.

Melting milky colors carried dirt away,
our cool joys delivered by a scrap-heap sleigh.

Summertime Cutoffs

Sheared from a school year's wholly-worn jeans:
Mother-made swimsuits, sport shorts, or any
all-purpose bottoms we needed for heated,
play-laden days and dusks. Chopped and ragged
above our dirty skinned knees: a frayed fringe
of loose-hanging threads once close-woven denim.

Lighter, longer, summer's strings unraveled
inch by tattered inch until our sunburned legs browned,
and our backyard sprinkler game time ran out.
Everything came undone in that unstructured season
sooner or later. Fall's brass fixtures buttoned up
our fun, heralded winter's coming covered pale skin.

Luna Moth Summer

Curious but cautious, we dared not touch
that great, grey-green Luna moth attached
to the camp store's screen door. "They only live
twenty-four hours," the ranger said, "then they're gone."

You, eleven, and I, thirteen: too old
to play, too young for wisdom that week
at the mountain retreat our parents had chosen
for us. We explored trails, felt waterfalls,

traded secrets until there were no more
unspoken words, except half-hearted farewells.
The moth remained, we made a plan to feel
beauty just once before parting. A quick

count to three, extended fingers trembling,
a sensual stroke of stiff silken wings
that spiraled to the wood-plank porch floor
like a leaf that found autumn too early.

Miss Bernice's Lesson House

Even the fingertip-pricking
desert cacti outside her hothouse
plastic-wrapped porch thirsted
there in year-round summer.

No A/C, but a time-ticking Galaxy
fan with hopeful transparent blue blades
oscillated low-tempo brief breezes
over her sweating piano students.

Every good boy did fine, but I
was never quite good enough –
more interested in all cars
eating gas, all cows eating grass.

Red pencil marks she'd make on mistaken
sharps and flats matched her hands' scratches
treated with ungraceful Swan merthiolate –
wounds torn open by her crusty-eyed feline.

Behind horned owl glasses, she inspected
imperfection: "Don't slouch! Hands off
the wood! Quit embellishing!"
Her tiny place free from put-on airs.

By the Steinway, a weak-legged table was
burdened with the bible and bottles:
large-letter labeled medications,
practices three times a day.

Tongue Economics

Danny Tillman eats [MF]ing mayflies for a quarter.
He waggles thin lips, [F]ing fake-chews, jaw bobbing,
then gulps as if [GD] dish soap tastes better.

His minister father believes in Palmolive
punishment: purifier, reminder, spirit-cure
for boys who take the Lord's name in vain.

A little green dab on tainted taste buds cleanses
sin and sugar-stained palates, color-coated
by twenty-five-cent machines' bubble gum – forbidden

sweet chasers to purge, forgive and forget flavors:
[SOB] bugs and betrayals for silver.

Scene from Rural Route Bus 43

We used our breakfast breaths to create white
canvases from windows in our school bus.
Our fingers drew love that faded in sunlight:
hearts and initials connected by crosses.

That was before the Howard Lee incident.

...*white trash idiot!* we heard Rhonda roar
at him from her corner seat, normally his.
Howard screamed back sausage-smelling curses,
threw his Bush Hog ball-cap into the aisle.

We'd never seen his greasy hair before.

He grabbed each side of her double-chinned face,
shoved her head through the back glass pane
affronting the fat fire extinguisher
and a red reflective emergency exit.

My God at all the blood. All over.

...*like a stuck pig!* my classmates said later
when Howard and Rhonda were off our bus.
Still, we held in affection's exhales,
kept our fingers clear of the windows.

Rising Student

Junior high's cracked concrete steps made us
practice, repeat the imperfect
ascents from sidewalk innocence

into faux knowledge: adolescence
leapt toward using hopscotch jumps,
double-dutch dexterities developed
on an easier, earlier playground.

Everyone busted it once, at least:
spilling books and dignity,
skinning knuckles, knees, and noses
in a duck-and-dodge, left-right hurried
ballet to beat the bells and odds.

They never made it quite right.

After dashes and dances, somehow
we managed to master those flaws
in the adult-made way that tripped us,
taught us firsthand about scraping
by, slowing down for those who refuse
to change or repair much of anything.

The Adolescent Litmus Test

"Today, class, we will learn how spies used
simple household lemon juice as a method
to invisibly transfer information to their allies,
and how this technique worked."
—*Mr. Potter's 6th grade science class lecture*

You had to have heat
to expose what I meant
through innocent, invisible
ink notes passed, penetrating
an upward-slanting locker vent,
or tucked into your waiting purse,
slipped from the zipper of my
bookbag's pen-swollen pocket.

Junior high's bittersweet period
sullied our prior years of friendship.
My mind's eye watched your naked
light bulb or candle flame warming
platonic lemon juice letters –
"Meet me by bike rack" or
"Lunch room food sux" became
burning anthems of things bigger,
deeper than acid-based lab tricks
infusing biology
with natural chemistry.

Hideouts' End

J-Byrd, Hank and I took to the woods
that summer when junior high ended.
Our wickiup: a lean-to dome
of broken oak branches covered and woven
in palm fronds and fragile Spanish moss
of one final childhood vacation.

Outside our shelter, J-Byrd's hatchet, Hank's fire,
and my slow-flowing creek gave us all
the reminders of endings we needed.
Inside, our put-away boyish things:
squirrel rifles, sheath knives, Daniel Boone daydreams.

A little bank mud, some tying green vines,
and there in the clearing it stood: our trio's
last common camouflage monument.

It stayed for a while even after we left
it – our Boy Scout bindings and redneck riggings
held fast until that hurricane season
when our structure fell victim to nature:
girl-named storms that blew everything apart.

The Last Lawn Boy

I yes-ma'amed her into eventual silence:
short and spectacled Mrs. Malcolm, whose stubborn silver
push mower never started on the first yank, paid the slow kid
before me double my ten-dollar half-acre rate.

Her quaking pointer finger matched her voice's tremble:
"Use plenty of muscle. My Hal always turned hard
to keep things neat and even. That's how they taught him
in the army, you know." I didn't. It didn't matter.

A downhill job: I had to level every blade
to please her Thursday sewing circle.
Never mind the soldier-straight edges –
her tips were delivered in dry-throated scolds:

"Don't touch my impatiens," and "Sweep the pavement," and
"Drink from the hose, young man," finished with "If
my husband were here," prompting my adolescent
resignation a few weeks into summer.

Her driveway was shaggy that July night
the ambulance blinked up to her door. I blamed
myself for cutting her off too soon; one or two
more runs might have meant room to breathe.

Veterans' Day: I visit the graves of my greats
when the coveralled caretaker comes, weed-eater
murmuring dirges to the Malcolms' nearby plot –
a trim too short, a pass too quick into autumn dusk.

Family Gathering

Dedicated to all my country cousins

In those Thanksgiving woods we were grateful
by nature, we were farm kids – mud-made
battle plans detailed our attack:

mounting our gallant oak-limb steed,
we hurled barrages of pine-cone grenades
followed by Sabal Palm frond spears,
then went hand-to-hand with sword sticks
in the friendly fire of safe conflict.

Wounded, the unnamed invisible invaders
cowardly crossed the creek, high-tailed
into town, where all of our dangers went
to regroup and plot their revenge against
us, the adults of tomorrow.

Writing for Mary

Mrs. Orwig's Tenth Grade English Class, 1991

Butterfly light, it warms my shoulder: your gaze
passes onto the page my fingers have filled
with cursive your mother taught me years before,
figures rounded here and now for your attention.

Your baseball-player ape boyfriend can't read
it. Seated beside you, he envisions home runs –
circling every base, his vulgar cleats
tear into white lines, cross the pristine plate.

Blue loops: my script matches, meets your eyes.
Sweeping, flourished curves of shared connection:
elegant, swirled ink answers on the sly – my
quiet victory, this period's secret cheating.

To Jenny, Who Sold Me Her Lit. Book

I come across your name
from time to time, behind
The Minister's Black Veil,
or penned upon Bartleby
the Scrivener's measured
margins along with your fast-pitch
jersey number 9 inked in pink.
At Young Goodman Brown's Faith,
you've exclaimed "GO MOCS!!!"
but you never dot "i"
with a heart or scribe flowery
thoughts beside Browning or Auden.

Upon occasion, though,
you'll trade obscenities
in the Keys with Hemingway,
scrawl snakes with girly curves
near Dickinson's Narrow Fellow.

Today, the canon isn't
quite so hard like it was
on an unmarried frat boy
with testosterone A.D.D.
I don't glaze over in wonder
about the forbidden castle
of your dorm room's inner sanctum,
nor do Holmes and I use clues
such as game days to conclude if
your hair is worn straight or pulled back.

Yet I still have to half-smile
as I find your reminders
of that overconfident point
in my life, best distracted
by imagery from the hand
of a blue-eyed softball player.

Response to Artist-Roommate's Suicide Note

Taking the coward's way out,
I called the campus counselors,
turned the thing over to therapists.

It's taken me this long to write back.

Your pencil lead was dulled
when you wrote in thin print
a mist-gray graphite goodbye:

Words too light, too weak for permanence.

Sure, I've thought about it, too –
how to reach happily ever after
without the trouble of living.

Here's where the abstract meets the concrete.

That avant-garde professor killed
your hypersexual still nude figure,
deemed an oil-on-canvas failure.

Die Man Die. Your ultimate revenge

hangs life-sized in the studio
downtown facing the street
these days, where people slow to stare,

stunned by your image: fine, finished.

On Earning my Family's First Terminal Degree

I am last-born luckiest, not smartest
among these intellects. I cannot can
vegetables, drive standard, form
dog-ear dumplings by hand. Made
piecemeal with scraps – whatever stuck –
my sheepskins and long robes flutter,
filled by unschooled wiser ones' whispers:
That-a-way, boy. That-a-way.

THE LOVERS

Minutiae

In love, the little things become the big things.
— Anonymous

In the last days
of Intro Photography,
Professor Obrecht assigned
new cameras with instructions:

Make the microscopic massive –
I want bugs and pollen,
dust specks and table crumbs,
and I want them to be immense.

On the beach rocks, we met to turn
shells into landscapes. You
went first, your pointed shutter
finger busy as you framed:

You don't hold your fork right.
You nibble your nails.
You crack your knuckles.
You whistle too much.

I was just attaching a lens
when you shuttered *It's over,*
whereupon I dropped everything.
Metal, glass, and plastic debris

shattered into sea oats and sand weeds –
a jillion tiny remnants out of place,
perfect for your A-graded eight-by-ten,
black-and-white final.

Emergency Exit

That date night at my alma mater,
I proved a terrible romantic,
escorting you to my lover-boy landmarks:

Erin's balcony, Claudia's bench,
Nikki's veranda, Rebecca's fountain.
How do you know these places?

Before I could answer, I rushed
us up an unfamiliar, rusty
fire escape: uncertain steps shook,

bent beneath our ascent
to your landing, overlooking
that history-filled campus

seen anew that night with you
from a creaking, trembling staircase.

Apology to her Daughter

I was one of many men
in and out of your mother's
life – dinner turned to midnight
encounters, and meanwhile you
suffered: instability
is horrible on children,
I now, as a father, know.

You're probably in college
by now, you don't remember
me: that stranger who never
tried to play daddy – just came
by your place for home-cooked rice
and chicken suppers followed
by dessert and desertion.

I have no excuses, no
"I was young and foolish" lines.
Today all I can offer
is this sorry "I'm sorry,"
a small and inadequate
tardy bandage for old wounds,
white scars pure as forgiveness.

Rain Check

"I'm going out to check the rain," he states
as if even weather needs his approval –
everything has his inspection to pass.

He means, of course, the gauge: graduated glass
tube catching sky-water and hope for crops,
crispy-thin and dry from a starving season's heat.

Staring down the hot dinner she made, she waits
for his return, for their communion
growing cold from unfulfilled anticipation.

"Three solid inches!" from the porch he at last reports.
Shucking shoes, hanging his hat, he settles
in for an unblessed supper, consumed alone.

Biological Warfare

Our mixed grasses natural patchwork lawn
drives our master-gardener neighbors crazy:
Their plush, groomed Floratam St. Augustine butts
up to our clover-pokeweed-chokeweed carpet
of shaggy, raggedy accident-flowers.

Midnight irrigations grow our native
species taller, thicker: green sulfur flames
make botanical Hell for the meticulous
inch-counters next door, grass shears in hand,
on their knees pleading for perceived perfection.

They summon uniformed men with laser-level
precision mowers to impress their friends:
Wine-drunk orchid aficionados
and tea rose tabulators who measure status
using their sloped nose-bridges as rulers.

We sit on our evening porch and watch
as spontaneous blooms close up for the night,
awaiting morning dew and light to rouse them
from their passive-aggressive slumber
to flourish in one more day's rebellion.

Life Support

I'm hooked to three machines, and you
and my mother are arguing out
of courtesy: "You take the recliner;
you need to sleep." That's all I can do

after the seizures and ensuing
brain bleed that got me choppered
here: the big-city hospital where men
on scaffolds outside the ninth floor

clean smog-clouded windows. I lie unresponsive
to your exchange with Mom, who dabs
with wet white cloths the dried froth
from around my lips – crusted palaver.

The wind picks up, the cleaners
grow sea legs, and you close
the blinds on the high, bright world.
I open my eyes to the dark.

Family Album, 2004

Like bent spoons turned to wind chimes,
we flattened and reshaped
our selves in lessened bed space
consumed by nature's disturbance:
that season of three hurricanes,
our firstborn inside you rolled and stretched.
Late into night, the neighbors' bamboo
shrieked its rubbing, bending cry
through our bedroom windows' plywood:
green cylinders' wind-pitched friction.

Circular saw-blades of weather
passed. After-storms' satisfied
sounds: final bands' thick drops fell,
settled into our new routines –
feeding, changing, quieting.

Shadow Box

Almost overnight,
the neighbors nailed up
a high wooden
plank-on-plank fence.

They'd heard the news
she was expecting
and they wanted no part
of the comings and goings
brought with an infant life.

Fetching the paper,
they'd scowl at her husband
as if he had broken
the homeowners' code:

just mow your lawn,
take your trash to the curb,
but making additions
is strictly *verboten*
by muted community rule.

There never were cries
or late-night store drives
no cradle, no bottles,
no pink or blue nursery.

The cold-quiet arrival
of afternoon mail
brings her the thick slabs
of hospital bills, emergency
loss reminders.

That monumental fence
remains – shielding next door
from what wasn't and isn't:
an absence with no need for boundaries.

Robins Come Early

As you gathered your things, headed
for your mother's, I counted eleven
on our dead lawn. February wind,
stiff as a construction paper heart,
held everything in pause – sunset
bird breasts glowing their orange
opposition to past-fall brown –
crowns, backs, eyes. Finally wings
burst boughward as our screen door's
report ruined every last
chance of this winter ending.

3 a.m. Mockingbird

His high-low taunts
helped us forget
gnawing, scratching
springtime attic rats.

With up-down cries
he sought to mate
in the humid dark,
alerting us out

of repeated dreams:
unpaid bills coming
due in all the wrong ways.
We could not obey

his full-chested message.
You rolled toward the clock,
I stared at the slow
ceiling fan. Shallow sighs

nothing like passion
from the feathered throat
boasting too late, too early
atop our too old oak.

First Marriage

Our public smile: that white picket fence
bordering our domestic life.
The moss and vines smothered it now,
and killing time was at hand.

Saturday always meant work to do
with tools and gloves; I began
chopping out the wild invaders –
knotted, tangled Virginia Creepers.

I could hear you inside, raging
at children, clutter and chaos
as usual, at your wits' end
over juvenile, minor matters.

And I, on the outside, fought
my bleach-bucket, scrub-brush rebellion
against the algal, green-brown decay
of our whitewashed-pure security.

That pristine, perfect portrait
of stereotypical,
standard suburban success –
piked, protective, wooden white lies.

When I completed restoring
our image, passersby would note
"What a nice young family" again,
convinced by a happy façade.

From the front window, we watched that fence
erode, consumed from the inside out,
by black mold, a growing dark despair,
a slow and certain succumbing.

Morning Window Snail

Like you, I can't divorce myself
from this house, my burdensome shell.
Obligations press on our backs,
the saddled attachments of life.

Both of us aimlessly wander, leave
imperfect circular trails no one will follow
in our path – our blind antennae
aim us each toward a greater nothing.

Sunlight warms the glass beneath you
until your release – a free-fall
into the earth you first came from:
damp and dark flowerbed compost.

I close the drapes and shuffle toward
the silent kitchen. One more load
of unwashed dishes to start
my day: a pointless, empty spiral.

On Deciding to Build a New House

Too long we have lived with elder ghosts.
We feel their urges in door knobs and drawer pulls.
We turn window latches and light switches from them.

Our desire: Fresh handles and hinges darkened
by our little rituals' seizable legacies –
that one day the youngers might grasp our habits
and push toward their own simple levers.
We long to press spirits alone, all owned by us.

View from the New Place

Horizon like a freshly-cut key
from the unfamiliar hardware store:
All peaks and shiny valleys of jagged-toothed
openings, waiting for time and friction
to wear its points to smooth and effortless
second nature, like a reach into jeans pockets,
the flip of a well-oiled bolt, those flexes
and reflexes that tell us at last we're home.

THE HEIRS

Upon My Son's Naptime

I contemplate my greatest uncle,
whose speed bump knuckles dug trenches
in Nazi landscape, foreheads, and faces
throughout the era of World War II.

An 82nd Airborne Ranger, holding
a knife was one of the tricks he used
to stay alert while standing guard—its metal
clang, if dropped, would keep him awake.

Bearing his name, you fight against sleep,
clutching my finger like government-issued
security: your digits and palm grasp hard
that first joint, not quite the hilt of my hand.

I know you've arrived at your dreams when,
with a sigh, you allow the release
of my unscarred, peacetime appendage,
exchanging it for your own closed fist.

Sidewalk Chalk

Dusty, gritty business: driveway art
made with pastel thick sticks, chubby
tan fingers. You've drawn our family:

an enormous dad – me – beside medium mom,
but you and your brother are tiny
in comparison to our grown-up lines.

I kneel and draw the sun in the sky
above you, and some distant figure –
a tree, perhaps – to add texture and life

to this stark, stick-figure existence
you've rendered too accurately for me.
"Let's draw our house," I suggest, hoping

you won't choose cold cylinders of grey.

Predatory Lesson

That day the giant grackle snatched
up the baby duck from behind
its mother, out of a newborn line,
together on the porch we watched

helplessly. The yellow hatchling, clutched
to sharp-taloned death, was pecked
and pecked by a spike-beak, black
leaving no piece of life untouched.

Fingers pressed to lips, your eyes white-wide,
you embraced our two young sons close-tight
with trembling words: …*alright; it's alright*…
We all knew it wasn't. We headed inside

to comfort and safety, deadbolt-latched,
but no lock stopped the inevitable whys
from our pale-shaken, face-drained boys –
innocence devoured in one foul catch.

Newspaper Kite

You've given wings to your father's old words:
my journalism's wrapped around a cross
of store-bought dowels secured with office tape.
Fingertips blackened with contagious ink,
you make my craft your own with time and care.

Conflict and controversy: distant thoughts
tethered to earth by white twine of child's play.
Contentment carried by wind and kept aloft
with the dexterity of innocence:
my son, anchor and lifter of language.

Battlefield Park

"Our history is here, son: your ancestors
died on this piece of land centuries ago.
See their names on that big stone?" I cannot
get your gaze away from that playground
the city erected on this scarred, sacred site.

Gaudy purple-yellow contraption thrown up
amid these acres of war-torn ghosts
whose musket balls gave politicians the right
to assemble that obnoxious monstrosity
over our sacrifice-stained soil.

Three little blond girls in dresses start swinging,
cutting saber-shaped arcs of sunlight and giggles
through the free air beneath this fair sky,
and I am transformed in the moment
you go to join them – children of liberty.

Spirit Encounter

I could have worried that cold Hallows Eve
when we made it home from trick-or-treating
and there was that owl: unafraid, peering
from my dark study's square window ledge.
I didn't though. He was small, not at all

like those somber-faced great horned harbingers
of storybook lore – all death and wisdom –
more like a clay pot waiting for flowers,
an earthen vessel sheltered and shrouded
by warm bricks, mortar holding frosted glass.

Crouching like pranksters, creeping slow
as frightened field mice, we inched toward him.
Whispering, pointing, my two sons –
zombie and doctor – wanted him to fly.
He didn't though. His nocturnal eyes turned

toward us, pleading to remain
in that safe alcove on the cusp between
contented thoughts and threatening night.
We headed inside with our pumpkins full
of treasures from our neighborhood.

His silhouette stayed, backlit in yellow
shining streetlamp shades – a happy shadow
sighing and cooing, soothing us into
deepest happy-dream slumber where we
could not worry until All Saints' morning.

Memory Fish

You would not approach our wooded side yard
in your camouflage rolled-cuff overalls –
"Piranha River," you had named it despite
the lack of water or danger there;
its grey moss shade and black dirt path
made it just foreboding enough
for a three-year-old boy to steer clear.

Today you're knee-deep in the Chattooga,
tugging at line and hip-wader suspenders,
creel stacked full of gasping trout
whose frowning mouths mistook for a meal
your small, colorful piece of revenge
for toddler nightmares, fright-soaked sheets.
Tonight we'll feast on your deep-fried fears.

Dusk Catchers

"Mosquito Hawks," the old folks named them: dragonflies
hovering low over our twilight lawn.
You and your brother chase them, buzzing in circles
about the open grass, snatching at sunset air
vibrating in their crooked trails and your laughter.

Yards away, the neighbors plan their next purchase
as luxury cars glide past our small houses
leaving toxic exhaust, emblems and envy
strangling struggling, surviving suburbia:
BMW – Buying Means Winning.

What will you do if you catch one?
Once you have stared into its bulbous clear eyes,
felt its metallic shock, an almost-sting,
like the others, you'll let it go:
concluding that it's just another thing.

My Grandfather's Glenn Miller Record

Innocent soundtrack of war
complete with well-polished brass
contained on a long-play black circle
blasting bursts of smoky song
through my free, peaceful living room.

Ebony-barreled clarinets
with gleaming silver hardware
roll mellow notes like tumbling bombs
across the front lines: E, G, B,
innocent soundtrack of war.

Trumpets and trombones break quiet,
leading a charge toward finale
in a shiny metallic display
of bright and brilliant bravado
completed by well-polished brass.

Those lustrous medal days
have passed, but still we feel
the resonance, liberty's tremors
heard in throats of instruments
contained on a long-play black circle.

Scratchy percussion: vibrations
measuring discordant harmonies
from chambers locked and loaded
with the power of human breath
blasting bursts of smoky song.

My young sons enter and listen
to a conflict-and-victory medley
that feeds their curious courage
with audible history winding
through my free, peaceful living room.

Natural Education

Nine-year-old boy, I've taught you
mating season calls for squirrels:
thumb pressed over curled index finger,
mouth on that hard line between them –
sharp chirps, quick chatter to lure
flourishes of brown-grey bush-tails.

Twelve-year-old boy, I've caught you
lying on your bedroom rug, girls'
imaginary lips made with bigger digits
in that same formation, but tilted
like you've seen movie couples do.
Saturday night is your first dance.

What we old men sometimes forget,
you young men always figure out.

Angling with Son from Drowned Friend's Spot

Your last saltwater fishing trip before college,
we return to Henry's pier near the lighthouse –
no boat, no brother, just us, bait and tackle.

You're over past hatreds of sticky, squid-smelling
fingers, ripping open a frozen square pack
with a sure blade and muscled forearms. You pass me
severed tentacles, crack dirty jokes. Your laugh: deep, dry.

Again I've forgotten something: this time water
for the sun-pounded point where we squint, reel, thirst.
Ever the father, I go get it for us both.
Over my shoulder, I glimpse you, thirty-years-younger
me, by yourself. We long for your blond brother.

Mother-Daughter Kayaking

Rotating black double-bladed oars,
our two flesh-colored elliptical kayaks
unite us in a separate, mutual quest:
circumnavigation of this lake.

Wheeling paddle motions past your girlhood
park with low rounded slides, baby-safe swings,
monkey bar dome where higher-voiced boys clambered,
merry-go-round where you lost an early tooth.

Curving with the shore's sweeping arc, we slow
our approach to the landmark hospital:
its floors packed circuits of sickness, hurt.
In the cardiac unit's cool shadow, I'm

pausing as you keep left-right pushing
toward a darkened marsh that conceals
an inlet only you know, close
to our destination dock, our point of start and stop.

Her Favorite Uncles

As the only child of only children,
she imagines her uncles: men
who smoke pipes, grow beards,
call her "sugar" at Sunday dinner,
and who always, always
remember her birthday
with ponies and dollhouses,
the things that her sole parents
would never think to do.

These uncles, who she assigns
all J names: Jack, Joe, John, James,
carry hard candies in their pockets,
slip off to the yard to pick kumquats
after lunch, and flash their pocket watches
to see if their time is up quite yet
as her pink and polka-dotted room
grows up, and makes monochrome ghosts
of what once were spectral figments.

Girl Sherlock

For my inquisitive niece

With Scooby-Doo flashlight and Nancy Drew fantasies,
she's checking every crevice and dark space
for those trick passageways old houses like ours
promise – hidden in hallways, concealed in closets.

Her nose for clues is smudged with crawlspace dirt,
fingerprints blacken with attic-aged dust,
forehead sweat drops on our summer sun porch,
her soft knees pink from searching the front sidewalk.

Discovery waits near the future's fireplace.

By suspicious loose bricks, at last she'll find
escape in that exact spot where she thought:
Through the study's sturdy wood bookcase,
with a pull of each spine, those levers reveal

secret steps to the mystery's conclusion…
Pages chart footsteps to her destination
chambers away from this humble homestead –
a path lit by flashlight under blankets at bedtime.

THE ELDER

Middle Class American Proverb

or The Modern Polonius

Seize victory in the just-getting-by.
Mow the weeds short and they'll look like grass.
Groom life's junk until there's content.
Pile armfuls of sweet-sweated darks, lights and brights.
Plant fork forests in the dishwasher basket.
Write finger verses in corner table dust.
Draw stars and smiles in bathroom mirror fog.
Vacuum love notes in hallway carpet.
Leaf-blow your name in the driveway.
Celebrate survival in everyday riches.

A Portrait of the Professor

Cycling to campus on an antique green three-speed,
he ponders the meaning of morning nothing:
omnipresent, overshadowing oaks and old,
overgrown sidewalk's irregular rhythms.

Done for decades, his dual-circuit routine
carries that same surety as shoulder strap's
press into fall flannel with word-weight:
his own, his idols', letters black and blue.

Pump and whir of grades beneath him – inclines, declines,
pavement malformed by rounded roadside roots
grown too big, too deep in this college town
moved into then out of by everyone else.

He returns at day's end to a lone easy chair,
its solitary yellow lamplight, and happy
static crackle of black vinyl white noise –
the sound sense of thirty-three rpm spinning.

Caladiums

Hearts or shields? He couldn't decide
the shape of those broad leaves.
After mother's fall, he'd buried their bulbs
around the side yard's stepping stones.

She loved the finches' dodging flitters
there – their free diving bursts
in the living black cool
afternoons dimming toward night.

Pink-red faces, green-veined in the shade,
sprung upright umbrellas to light
the round rocks once too dark
for her feeble feet to find.

He watches her traverse that trail
marked by his labors, countenances
creased yet bright. He recognizes
now their familiar form: spades.

Labyrinth Keeper

Trinity-Grace Episcopal Church; Cloverdell, NC

He comes to the garden alone,
tending its encircling green hedge-walls
with kind clippers, fine trimmers
of a master's hand, assuring
no Babylonian confusion
besets the tranquil wanderers
in this intentional wilderness.

No Minotaur here, no golden calf-
man roaming to slay the lost souls.
At the growing heart, a cross:
serene in its silent symmetry,
giving wayfarers, trail-finders,
path-followers the rest
none other has ever known.

Birthday Beard

It draped my aging face beneath naked
stars, waxing moon, night's heavy warm throw.
I marked my sixtieth year on the island of summer
by growing that Robinson Crusoe beard.

It unfurled, wild and ragged, curling its fronds
into the tropics, seeking its place, longing to belong
among the aging truths that were. No Socrates
or Whitman wisdom arrived with it. Its unexamined
life bushed and spread until zephyrs passed a song
of myself through its strands – untamed harp-strings
breathed upon by saltwater seraphim and humidity.

Its vines stretched and climbed until they frayed. Fall approached.
My kayak cut the water back toward the mainland.
There, I'd bare my countenance into civilized winter.

Railroad Spike Dreams

Centuries I sat flat and sharp, keeping time,
holding track between mines and mines.
Hard-handled hammers rang me into this bed;
with each heated present-day engine's rhythm
I rise – inching taller and looser.

Some soon caboose, I'll shimmy free,
lie by the ties until her fingers find me.
She'll turn me over and around again
until she feels trust beneath my rust
and pockets me for her white window sill,

where vibration means she found a clear station
on the stereo playing lazy-day blues.

Dreams of the Dead

It's always so good to see them again: the late
great influencers of times and places expired.

They show up with full smiles, better posture,
bright fair skin their earth lives never gave them.

Occasionally, they're solely present in passing,
but often, there's a party they just couldn't miss:

elders embrace their great-grandchildren –
once divided, disconnected descendants.

Tragic-end friends arrive in pristine vehicles,
undamaged and sleek from streets of gold.

Aunts and uncles rejoin, bringing favorite
dishes – welcome changes from milk and honey.

Here, the festivities never end until
brain static and pillow scent call a halt

to parallel-universe celebration, ushering
in the living daylights of a woken world.

Meeting Frost in Paradise

I do not trouble him
with barreled talk
of rain or crows.

Walking is enough.

Green pastures, still waters –
only the divinest words
will do here, so we don't.

Walking is enough.

Questions? Yes, but not today.
Apples without sin
are in season, perfect.

Walking is enough.

As others climb the ladder,
we are here, where a square
and optional wood pile calls.

Walking is enough.

ACKNOWLEDGEMENTS

Greatest appreciation is expressed to the editors of the following publications, where some of these collected poems first appeared, though sometimes in a different form:

Big River Poetry Review – "Broken History"

Breath and Shadow – "Medicated Youth" and "The Tongue is a Flame"

The Chaffin Journal – "The Last Lawn Boy" and "Fraterville Central"

Dash Literary Journal – "Luna Moth Summer"

The Dead Mule School of Southern Literature – "Dusk Catchers," "Battlefield Park," "Memory Fish," and "Mule Pie"

Deep South Magazine – "Lovebug Seasons," "Family Gathering," and "Handcestry"

Emerge Literary Journal – "His Legacy"

FlaRe: Flagler Review – "Her Favorite Uncles"

Floyd County Moonshine – "Scene from Rural Route Bus 43"

FRIGG Magazine – "Upon My Son's Naptime," "To Jenny, Who Sold Me Her Lit. Book," "Where Our Tunnels Went," and "The Short End"

The Furnace Review – "The Left Farm"

Hobo Camp Review – "Everglades Requiem"

The Marjorie Kinnan Rawlings Journal of Florida Literature – "The Meaning of Wauchula" and "Family Gathering"

Miller's Pond Poetry Magazine – "Laundry Grading"

Real South Magazine – "Labyrinth Keeper"

Saw Palm – "End Weekend" (featured in "Places to Stand in Florida" section) and "Natural Education"

Steel Toe Review – "Tongue Economics"

Touch: The Journal of Healing – "Asperger's Syndrome: Day Fifteen," "Life Support," and "Response to Artist-Roommate's Suicide Note"

Town Creek Poetry – "Summertime Cutoffs"

The Wayfarer – "North Room Bedtime" and "Robins Come Early"

www.ingramcontent.com/pod-product-compliance
Lightning Source LLC
Chambersburg PA
CBHW031142090426
42738CB00008B/1189